Tears of the Drum

A Tears by the Gallon Collection

Jeffrey B-Izzaak

authorHOUSE®

AuthorHouse™
1663 Liberty Drive
Bloomington, IN 47403
www.authorhouse.com
Phone: 1 (800) 839-8640

Published by AuthorHouse 09/06/2017

ISBN: 978-1-5246-8570-6 (sc)
ISBN: 978-1-5246-8569-0 (hc)
ISBN: 978-1-5246-8568-3 (e)

Library of Congress Control Number: 2017904717

Print information available on the last page.

This book is printed on acid-free paper.

"The Island has a most beautyful appearance, and conveys the idea of one continued garden, finely diversified with hills and deep narrow Slacks, or Glens, interspersed with natural clumps of wood, whose soil has not been thought worthy of cultivation, which serve not only to ornament the face of the Country but likewise afford Shelter to the surrounding fields."

Visitor to Carriacou Sept 25th 1787

View toward Carriacou South from Belle Vue North, 2014.

From wattle and daub to the erection of concrete balusters. My tears spread like sheeted rain over your acres.

Tears by the Gallon

Aerial view of Hillsborough town, bay and environs (undated)

Hillsborough and its environs, 2017

Other books by the author:

Poetic Duty I- Coming From Carriacou (2013)
Poetic Duty 1.5: Without Definition- A Kayak in Englan' (2014)

The Drum Cry for CARRIACOU:

The drum, cry out in sorrow. The drum, cry out yesterday, today, and tomorrow. The drum exalts our joys, soothes our desperation, and keeps alive our celebrations.

How I crave your feeling, your every sense engaged, without reliance on these feeble efforts to depict, convey and transport you through. How I wish you could see the inhabitants and taste our emotions, pay attention to our conversations and appreciate the landscape in which this drama is cascading-unfolding. Take a glimpse of the invasion, the divisions.

How I wish I was a painter, and every stroke was a revelation, telling you the story, that would touch you, evoke your spirits; make you see Carriacou as it was in my eyes, and that of others, in this year- just before and thereafter?

'This is a place to be discovered
This is the Last Frontier.
All others conquered
Soon, the last bastion would fall
So we can hoist the flag
To our ancestors;
Intrepid explorers.
As for the locals
(We brought them here; to Aborigine and Maori there is no
compare!)
They'll remain dazed
Crazed
Bearers of our umbrellas
And carriers of our litters...'

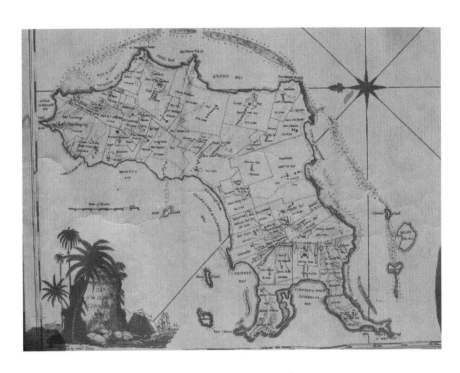

Copy of 1784 Map of Carriacou

CONTENTS

DRUM 1

Bula

On May 22, 1838, the British House of Commons passed a resolution 1838 putting a stop to the system of apprenticed labourers, and on the memorable First of August that year the stain of slavery on the British escutcheon was wiped away by the proclamation of complete emancipation of all of the enslaved subjects of the Queen in the West Indies. The conduct of the liberated people in Grenada on that day was most exemplary. They spent the early part of the day in their several churches, and then united in festive gatherings, but there was no drunkenness or disorderly conduct.

© The Grenada Handbook

SUNDAYS, CIRCA 1980's

B

There was Sunday mornings
Fireside, wood fire smoking
Yard fowl overnight in the pot cooking
Sunday morning
Cousin Veda dressing
Pulling up her stockings
The radio, Joseph Niles^ singing
Gospel music people tuned in

After the Revolution#
Evolution slowly come in
The faithful stop church-going
Unfaithful, but still wanting a blessing
Waiting, demanding
Now the days are not the same again

Nah

Can't hear Cousin Dear Me*
under the mango tree
So much love, so many darlings
The place overgrown
Now cows on the loose are the ones camping
Is a new- ism
Wireless express
Religion advertising
Catch Jesus on the wire
To wash away your sins
Log on
Log in
Ride the board bus
Or just walking

Father Anglican giving confirmation lessons and communion
New dispensation for the slave children
Take up the practice in profusion in the West by adoption
Not inheritance
Too late now to take the opposite stance
Sunday mornings are not the same
Again
^ Barbadian gospel singer
# The Grenada Revolution, 1979-1983
* Dorothy Gabriel, lived in Grand Bay while farming land with resident mango trees, in 'Along', Mt. Pleasant

U

DIS GENERATION
A livication to "Nyah Keith"

'Dis generation is one of scorch and burn
Fire!
When they done everything brown down
Give dem a few and then look back to see the mark
Ashes and stubble, no road, no track
Dis generation of millennials from the millennium
They don't care about knowledge or old time wisdom
Who is prime minister of St.Kitts and Nevis?
How and when did the breadfruit reach Kingstown?
Make it worse, they don't teach the revolution- Haitian or Grenadian.
Just cash and flash, give them in hand
They despise the land; they'll weed the grass with dot.com

Dis generation
Interested in wholesale of land
Don't care for grandparents; forget great, great, and if they eat their spit to keep intact the bound stone. 'For sale. For sale. Come one. All come.'

They come and meet it; it's not ours to keep. Just ah gift. Why you selling it?

Wah man! Is a conflagration. Sweeping heat. Arson. Arsonists in spirit. Ah look. Ah see it. You can't talk. You can't speak, to them. Everything. They already know it. When? How could you learn as a child if all your friend is children? Face de book. Read a new anthem.

"Cut yuh nails. Wash you hand. Grate the coconut. Wash you hands again. Squeeze it. Three times darling. We want to get everything. Come on. Wash you hand again. Burn you onion and garlic before you put in de peas and let it simmer. When de pot done you food go taste sweet." But you must be humble to learn. Respectful to older ones and you will profit.

They want money in a hurry
Instant is instantly
But what you expect really?
Born under electric light is electricity
Ladjablès nuh dey; and no fear of de Almighty
Dis generation done reach way dey going ahready
Buy de board, get some nails, build de coffin; when they dead they must get bury.

"I can't sell it, it doesn't belong to me. It's part of my heritage." **The 6th Duke of Westminster**

L

'Welcome home Wimpey'
Was introduced to Jeffrey on a yellow tee
Somewhere in the region of a year after 1983

He thought it was a story of a pussy;
Not a mascot or letterhead for some company

The things we see, the things we think
The things we imagine, assume we know
While totally disconnected on a far-shore

Can wash up a beach we translate
Near us with a message not really meant for us

Like a cat on a yellow t-shirt
'Welcome home Wimpey'

A

I

If OUR society can be so petty, so narrow
To blossom OUR sorrow
WE end up like WE don't know
WE are related to the people
Who auctioned off St.Louis and portions of Bogles

Conversation in the cemetery
Can be like standing in a market beside the seashore
Oiled for sale like chattel
Depending on your point of view;
Don't be righteous, overly, like the ancient Pharisee
Do you know the pain of Dorothy*
To see her three pickney sold like birds in one day?

'Sorry.
Your history lessons won't do
If WE sell what we inherit
And return to work for the people we sell to,
What business is it to you!
You have a different idea?
Who are you lecturing to?
Boy, you too little
A! A!'

Big men travel to the Big Apple
Yet still talking trifle
The longer WE are confined to 13 Square Mile mentality
The more WE get stifle
Not enough time the answers to know
Before WE resemble the ground we walking on and turn to nutton.

* A name for the mother of Mary Prince, who was sold at age 12 for £38.00, along with her two sisters, Hannah and Dinah

"*When the sale was over, my mother hugged and kissed us, and mourned over us, begging of us to keep up a good heart.... It was a sad parting; one went one way, one another, and our poor mammy went home with nothing.*" **Extract from "History of Mary Prince, A West Indian Slave."**

D

II

In the cemetery to bid another valediction-
When you dead ahready, you done
One thing left is get bury
You hear me?
Ah say,
'The sepulcher four feet deep instead of six!
And what of all the families scattered in it?'

You can cup a hand of sensimilli ^
Or ride high on stupidity
One man talking control trying to convince me
While Donny reasoning on life and its mystery
Job a pawn in a Universal game-play
We know so much yet steeped in superstition and ignore-apathy
We better find answers before we dead anyway
But if you been dead before, you just have to return to bury

Cousin of mine say I look like Sir Eric Gairy#
Means nothing to me
A compliment? Maybe. As if I care?
If you have nothing to say then why go there?
Leh we enjoy mutton soup wid dumpling and drink some beer
Look at each other until we meet again in the cemetery
Next year?

^ Sentimental reference to marijuana
# Grenada's flamboyant and charismatic first Prime Minister

R

I

So now that you know my history
Is the despisation tangible retribution
A symbol of the repay?

EH?

Now that you know my first dwelling was a shack
(In Sierra Leone what was the Hut Tax?)
Do you feel confident I don't deserve all that?
So you think it is ok
And then you spat!

WHAT?

But I'm not in shock
After I gave you the right of away
To come here,
Roam free from Tiboud to Tiblee
So you can tell me the trails you know intimately-
I have no idea;
Now you've acquired your desired
From me through familiarity
Your contempt
I reap every day?

YEAH!

I just wish I could say
It was that way in Philly
Atlanta, Minnesota, Chicago,
Your big cities
Or France, Italy and Germany

'Migrants' who discover
Land of Coo-coo and Okro
The ideal place
For the modern economic
And peace seeking refugee

That you could see
We are your hosts
Open to our guests
Willing to share
Aware of our and your history
Belief in Jah Almighty
YEAH
True human dignity
And yes, we love Bob Marley
But it seems- isn't the evidence so clear?
That you don't see it that way?
Do YOU?

U

II

Because if Dolliah
Went as far as America
To get ring on finger
Across the colour barrier
While pushing freestyle afro
As if Black Lives Really Matter

Please
Ease off them ole time talk
How you remember
A wild son of Cousin Veda
Playing hide and seek in the grass
In de pasture

As if Carriacou remained stagnant
While your travels to wherever
Opened up so many new vistas

Nah nah nah nah!
Don't placate-we need no apology
Is here we dey
Intend to stay
And we nuh sorry
Come for Regatta
And then make your way
Come in November
Light your candles
And leave Carriacou
Fuh we
Who see her in a different way.

What ah shame!
All these children
Desert their home
Would not turn around
To erect a new reality
Promoting ancient civilizations
Miracle economic stories
To make we feel bad
Because we so ent been no way

III

And if Merle
(Oh girl, you haven't aged an ounce since that day!)
Returned home only to turn away
And revoke her birthright and residency
Because of a new generation
Behaving the wrong way
Who is me to say?

To try explain the origins?
If it is grandparents missing
Or children making children
Or we just thinking we the last of The Mohicans
A soon to be extinct species
Then why give in prematurely
To these children?
It will be theirs soon anyway
But don't just give it to them
For free
Fight dem!

M

GANJA TRIPS -THE GRADUATION

The Class of 2010 graduated
To a Higher Grade
Way, way, up dey
And not shy to blaze
And halo in the haze
Firewood, lighter or strike by the sea
No discrimination,
Full-time enrollment
Full-joy consequence
Land of Liberty...
My surprise on the rise
'Dread, you mean is everybody
Ah didn't know
A, A'
It's high grade parade
Elders and teenage
On the weed thoroughfare
Without a care- paper, corn straw, scissors
Tongue glued by saliva
Ready to use...
'Excuse me, I'm going to make smoke...'
'I can cope, why the apology?'
Without diplomacy
To be
Most definitely.
Everybody graduate
With vested authority
And despite detractors
And their dismissive summary
In the vein of Jeffrey on holiday
From NE USA
Ganja trips

Now barely necessary
The grass has fully grown
Found a home
Established residency
I'm stoned
Don't know how to interpret the visual
Or what to say...

B

STONEMAN IN RESIDENCE

I

For now
I own these stones-
Icebergs in the sea of this island
Stained by the weathering
Of white cedars on a plateau
That on afternoons
Cast shadows across Sabazan
I am the man; no other one
Forever and for as long in my imagination

The barbed wire imbedded in trunks
Bent, rusting, posts now defunct
Gardens perhaps
Cotton I imagine
Most dissolved into time
Save for the signals
Evolved with time
To remind us:
We own everything
And nothing, same time

And let the stones be silent
They are the real resident

II

RESURRECTING LIONEL
For 'Stoneman' Lionel

Lionel, the fire man,
Jeffrey thought about you in derision
Until this morn
Rounding the corner
Buffeted by Atlantic streams
Your handiwork, a greeting,
Lionel, in resurrection.

Charcoal, wood, leaves,
Your weapons.
Shrubs, stumps, trees,
Mornings and evenings,
A fiery destination.

Maudlyn in her decayed beauty
Still has the relationship
With her cigarette
And wild hungry dogs as pets
Her face a reflection of fire inside
Dark, burnt, ashes,
Sometimes like the house in which she lives.

The grass was burnt black and brown
The trees still stood
But your dedication was relentless
Everything erased
Then another time
Before you can rest
And you never did.

U

APPEALS #1 and #2

"L'Esterre
21 October 1967

His Lordship,
The Chief Justice

Sir,
Having due respect for the very high esteem and idealistic principles
established in democracy and British Jurisprudence, I wish to draw
to your attention being a layman, what I term a misdemeanor in Her
Majesty' court of Justice..."

Hillsborough
21 September, 2016

Your Most Excellent Majesty,

We your subjects long forgotten
Think it not reprehensible
To appeal to your Most Benevolent Mercies
To visit or send representation to witness
What has become of we
In the District of the Northern Magistracy

Your portrait framed by your heirs
Hangs beneath the broken AC Condition
Discolored by time's traverse
Not a representation worthy of your elevated status
And the children have since grown!

Bless your subjects of Canada
However, the pillars are fractured
The ceiling low

Fluorescent tubes in dual rows
As Royal Officers lined-up
For early morning inspection
The air is warm
Fans white like the ceiling but not spinning
Left only for the one standing
That cannot differentiate variations of temperature

Your Excellent Majesty,
Positively,
The benches are new
Fuh true
Reminiscent of seating in a church pew
New coat of varnish
The laws of Grenada-10 volumes
Black, hard-cover monuments in constant revision

Silence.
Brown envelopes.
White paper.
Flag of Grenada.
Counsel for the Defense.
Two-striped Corporals.
The Bailiff-
White shirt, black tie-
Phones in obedience abide.
We await the entry of His Honour
It's not too late
To give us some cool air
So your subjects can breathe
A little easy
Now that we are free
The lawyers persecute
It's all we
But Your Majesty,
The years have absolutely expired

While in some ways
We find ourselves mired
In stagnancy...
So please come and help we

L

23/9/16
Dumfries:
5:50 am

Lagoon of Hope

There is a Lagoon of Hope in Dumfries
That offers dispatch for my disappointments, limitations, unexplored
confined fallacies.
Just beyond black and bleached pebbles smoothed
Where villages once sacrificed to gods unknown
While dry season raged.
And now truckers violate the sands
A rape exposing the few stands of mangrove that remain

In this new dry season
When the waters of life recede in rapid evaporation
And juveniles darting with abandon
My hope, my joy, soarings too, evaporate
And lie baked on the dry earth

But never forever- never for long
Because the thunder and rains would awaken
And the basin welcomes the flood
Dormant cells sense their time for resurrection
The common Terns would skirt and glide, harvesting between tides
Dragonflies - bombers with erratic flight patterns,
Madden the pre-sunrise stillness
Mangroves kissing at the interface of water and sky

And so too go my hope
With the cycles of the seasons
From depression to ecstasy
Death to rebirth
It happens, on the shores of Dumfries
As it does in places sacred and secret to worshippers
Across this island
In consummation with their hopes.

A

JI-FREY AND SOLOMON'S ODYSSEY

Like the king in Jerusalem
I embarked on this journey
Of discovery of me
Suspending my imagined advances
Subtracted from all normalcy
On a sabbatical
I took a holiday
To see what I would see new to me

I wanted to know
Why no one said
Or read
Where were the quotes of the great ones who wrote?
Or was I being ungrateful
Too aloof and so miss
The force of simplicity and purity
Of unfolding in a small-island community?

How far would it take me?
How big was my pond?
But I must explore this odyssey
Even if it returns me to square one
I need to meet the kings of Persia in modern day Iran
The royal princes of India
Travel the realms of Afghanistan
Explore the libraries of Timbuktu
Live for 10 years
A subject in the Songhai Kingdom

Because I've been so cheated
All the connections I need to live

Tampered with or deleted
And you expect me
To accept your concept to rateed?
But to lose humility
For the full parade
I'm afraid
Look!
If I'm a child of the universe
Then I deserve to know
How the universe was made

Like the king in Jerusalem
I want to know what life is –
Reality? Or make believe charade?
I want to meet the Queen of Sheba
And her entourage
Witness the full cortege
But I'm too busy
Searching for meaning
And the conclusion
To be up in my chamber
Reclining near the horizontal
As if getting laid.
Instead I'll rise to say...

"GOOD MORNING!"

From windows facing the sea
I pursue an ever shifting exhibit of the mornings
In a sea of constancy
That makes me believe
That I am alive again
As the intensity of the sun
Presents fresh canvas on which to elucidate my art

A daybreak rising from a night embracing the dew
A passage without lines;
Left of the cliffed-shoreline
Tears in silence at the erosion
My inaction, across the road to Sabazan
In the gathering shade of the big tamarind
I glimpse Jean for Champion
The reflection from her means of transportation
Reassures me.

"Good morning Jean!"

They've returned-
same boat, same spot,
Fishing my sea without permission
'Don't stay, go away'
To a place where
I am unaware
But before you start the engine

"Good morning,
I see you!"

Some times
I am disappointed, excited, jealous
Sometimes, they visit in combination
Or in quick succession
I gaze out the window,
I stand,
I try to gauge the tides
I sweep across Dumfries Bay
To see the water mark
Is it full?
Is it going down?
Can I explore?
And if everything is ok

I have other plans
Embrace my excuse
Take another look
Breathe

And say, 'Good morning
Look me here!'

A WAILING IN LACA PIERRE

They wail and lament every morning
They lament and I'm powerless to help them
Akin, I imagine, to their foreparents children
To release their parents from the whip and the chains
Powerless, because they carry your name
In a time far removed from the Burning Spear' refrain:
'Mommy, mommy, mommy, mommy, mommy, mommy, mommy...
Please don't beat the little children so hard.'

They wail in their yard
No quarter for rescue
They wail on ignorance mixed in the wet clay of anger toxic coming
through
Every fall of the cruel bramble
Without option, but you are nursing a rising rebellion
In Laca Pierre as did Napoleon in San Domingue
Don't beat the lil children so hard daddy.

They will imprecate you in silent resolve
And as their world revolves you lose the slave master's control
Emancipation or guerilla warfare- burn this plantation down...
Tomorrow Friday begins,
And if I hear their voices raised again, then it means, you're not
listening
'Mommy mommy mommy mommy mommy mommy! Please don't
beat the children so hard.'
Or like the children of Abraham, they would be heard by God and
you will go the way of Pharaoh

AND, INTRODUCING MALCO:

Malco,
Flowing from Maracaibo
Through the flood waters of the Orinoco
Nash planted a seed
And it grew into Malco
Transplanted on Carriacou.
Monday morning
Green fig skin touching discarded dumplings and
Coconut husk dehydrated become united in a Velvo Kris margarine tin

'Malco!
You feed the pig?'
'Yes,
Pig fat, fat, fat
As tief'

Skip Tuesday
To the end of the week
After grass feeding in the morning
Friday about seven
Boys are ready
On tour with their chores
And so is Malco
African blended Latino
The pig
Under the common cherry tree
Resigned
To wait and see
Weeks,
Months,
Until the day,
Because every pig
Must have its Saturday

'Malco!'
'Yes Tanty,'
'The pig ready?'
'Pig fat, fat
Fat like tief'

So you may think
Or find it strange
Or burst your brains
Shifting through a possibility range
And text on child psychology
When you walked the ten yards
Over hard rock
To gauge
The size of the pork stock
To the shock
Of bones and chains
The only leftovers
'No!
He did not!
Do that!'
And his words
Keep ringing
In your ear
Or somewhere

'Malco!'
'Yes
Pig fat, fat,
Fat like ah tief.'

DRUM 2

Cut

'We learnt to play the drums during breaks (while the players were having refreshment). Some [elders] didn't like it; but others didn't mind. "The boys of today would be the men of tomorrow. Leave them alone, let them play." '

Cut drummer of Mt.D'or

C

The confines of my limited grammar
Is like trying to explain
The delicate balancing act
Of overnight water – droplets extended on a blade of grass
My descriptive pronoun would be so misplaced
Like food without taste - warap*

I'm about to cross, traverse, the empty ravine
There is a concrete wall - black stones in the face of the facade
A barrier to temper Chapeau Carre's# seasonal spill-over
So what have I got to say?

The confines of my limited grammar
Renders these lines inferior; far from superior
It is so daunting an endeavor to try to capture
On pieces of paper
Scattered collections

Where do I begin?
What words do I author?
Wasting so many stanzas
And still not getting closer
Far away, so far
Even as I'm doing right yah
* Food lacking character
#Carriacou's 2nd hill of prominence

U

I wish I held command of handsome word interactions
Near relations to the introductions of Castaways on a Desert Island
by Kirsty Young
The marriages of convenience, subtle arrangements
That attracts your conversational palate...
'Come take a taste!'

I wish I could weave and conceive lines so pregnant and relevant
They would leave your expectation so heavy
That your colour would fade pale
Until they come forth and you exhale
With relief, excitement and disbelief

That I could sustain intensity
To imprison your attention
A thoroughly enjoyable lock-down
While expressions consume the room
Ascend and cascade down the walls of your cell
Travel inverted across the ceiling
Dancing around your light bulb...
And you would so yearn for more
Not because they are harbingers of peace
But purveyors of sweet release
And you'd be free!

Wishes and me
Since I admit defeat
As seen through Crystal's sheet
I am not in that sphere at all!
Sometimes I wish I could make it – that I confess.
Also, every time I try to rise
No sooner the elevation,
I plunge into deflation!

To

T

When the colonizers came
To eliminate and then sustain
Their future with black stains
In Dumfries, Craigston, Meldrum and Belvidere
Names like the salted things imported from Northern England –Scotland
To the said Urquhart* plantations of sugar and rum

Then a sudden departure as soon as it was all over
Peasants in huts, rags, bugs,
Dogs feeding off the meager extrusions from...

Black butts left landless, destitute
Scavenging squatters without work
Who would have predicted this return?
Without rifles, torture or powered gun
Less than 200 years on?

[A Methodist Minister via Wahhabi Medina-
Home of the Messenger – Peace be unto Him – professor from Oklahoma;
Who the hell was Timothy! He doesn't matter;
Outside the Lime Tower, opposite the gate of a Rasta.
Yes Iyah
Cutlass in hand- if you can see the picture
I'm a peasant too; the years cannot [profer]]
*Scottish family with estates in Carriacou in the 18th and 19th century

T

She gave her dollar to the gatekeeper and enter without the piece of paper
To collect black bags of lettuce and whatever
Shipped over from the islands- the new plantations-
And walk back out without reference or interference
While me, a former Custom's Officer,
Wouldn't dare to assume that I was entitled to such right of way
By virtue of my history, or the colour I used to bear

And I ask Jeffrey,

'What is wrong with me? Carriacou? We?
Our vision?
The things we can't see!'
Maybe it's our mentality
Inspired, conspired, by years under plantocracy:
'Keep locals waiting while visitors go free?'
Soon, this place could be
A mini Pretoria pre-1993.

She came with her camera
A mobile capture of Kayaks having fun
Missing others, lens focused on the people at home
Her copyrights given without their permission
While me,
An amateur lover of film photography
Would not dare behave that way
Among my own company

So I ask she,
'How could this be?
Who gave you the right?
What's your intentions?
Because they're unclear.'

But if we're all quiet: we don't see, don't hear
Our images can be altered
Worse, photo-shopped out of here!

She nodded her head
Lips pointing in my direction
'It's for the locals; them is why we give an extra one.'
I imagine scorn, I see derision
No respect. But on whose demand?
'Keep smiling'
That's what the law demands
While me
Whose navel string deep in Newland* dutty
Can't buy a slice at 20.33
But as I go around
I see these ladies in Town, Tyrell Bay, L' Esterre
And I tell you
More than me, they must be born right here!

Ps: It doesn't get better
She came at the dawn of evening
Dressed in shorts, walking,
Shears in hand...
'What's your intention?'
But she wasn't saying
As if I was the invisible man looking!
Retrieved her collection and began the pretense
'Is that your garden?
'Do you plant corn?'
* Northern ridge joining the heights of Belair to Mt.Pleasant

E

"...to the people, who are prone to imitation." **A Reference to the people of Carriacou in a Colonial report, 1903**

DEPRIVED KAYAK

I became jealous of Europe and its history
In cathedrals to Christianity
Monuments, scientific discovery
Palaces, castles, museums of display
Literature, art, bars of Mozart, Bach and Tchaikovsky

I became convinced
That if I didn't absorb the masters –
Yeats, Elliot, Shakespeare, Wilde, Chaucer,
And learn Greek philosophy –
Pluto, Aristotle, Socrates, Parmenides,
I would be confined to shallow backwaters
A victim of intellectual poverty

My soul became
Enveloped by grief
To find that I am from
A generation that missed
A grammar school education
The discipline of colonial and religious headmasters
Royal Readers, drama, music...
That I imagine would have bequeath me
A well-rounded periphery

So I led a rebellion
In the shadow of Julien Fedon
Raiding my experience-plantation

Holding those of all age captive
Children, women and man
In my mountain stronghold
I would only release you
On the meeting of my demands:
Change the year I was born!
Change the location!
Move the year of independence!
My classroom!
Village associations!
Move calypso!
Move Big Drum!
I don't want to
Spend this currency
Change my whole journey!
And bring me near Europe
So I can cope

R

Ps PLUS

Carriacou?
What's your Foundation?
Where did it spring from?
Do you have a plan, for those who return
To become the new owners of your island?

You see,
Can we sell out land,
For biscuit and jam
And end up six feet deep
In cemeteries bequeath...?
Who is going to beat our drums?

Nah man!

Wah man!
Who is walking down your street?
Who lays claim?
Who owns it?
Are these circumstances replete
By the flip of a coin switch
Where we would greet you in our arms...?

"Money is the biggest temptation, but the land is not a thing to be sold. It doesn't matter that we are not rich... I will never sell out the land because people are important and land is important for the future." **Island Chief, Solomon Islands**.

Across the way to Kasav, 2016

D

'Return to Carriacou?
What for?
What to do?
To sit and watch waves collapse on Kasav*?
One tree, one wind
Filling sails of galleons
Transportation for hapless humans
Imprisoned on an ocean by the sea?
Are you really crazy?
Asking me to retire
And spend the rest of my days
With that shadow over me?'

'Besides,
I have no feelings of affinity
And I hear the residents
Have disposed of the unity
We've come a long way from huts
To a full embrace of modernity
But I don't care
Carriacou is not for me!'

In these tiny cathedrals of our scope
Limited as our visions are
To the rim of the island's horizon
In months when storms of gale force
Clamour across reef-protected lagoons,
Joining forces with currents running long
Some rising from the Orinoco basin
As turbulent as the Serpent's Mouth...

We the citizens on the Forgotten Isles
Are remiss of the wider sweep
Of the waters in which we lie
And that other
Which borders lands afar:
Africa, West, Portugal, St.Helena
So many stories to populate landscapes
Stories rich and deep, mundane and desperate,
Stories incomplete;
Suddenly severed from the earth
The horizon, the seasons;
And we forget we are not near
The only ones- just an illusion
Isolated in our minds
In reverse for better;
Often for a lot worse
These islands above 12 Degrees North

If I were...
I would do something
Different from the storms that sometimes visit
Most a miss
Few, like Janet#, a hit
So potent that hearts would rend
And be bent by forces stronger than created evolution
Residents would find a new perspective from which to view their island,
'Not for sale!
Not one inch!
No!'
* Appearing as Cassada Rocks on maps
# Hurricane of 1955

R

WRITING EPITAPHS

I

Epitaphs we construct
Stories by the million
Glory and infamy
Most shrouded
Few in mystery
But we draw, carve, hew,
Search for appropriate effect in reflections.
On this day we lay beneath umbrellas-
Mostly black
Braving this unseasonal January downfall
The victim, a resident of Mt.Royal
I could not outline
What makes the script special
"Amazing Grace"...
What does death save us from?
Human debilitation?
Irreconcilable complications?
To succumb
So that the surviving ones
Can write epitaphs?

Names deleted

II

Ovid, Argyle, Endeavour, Dingwall
Are names now lying dormant
Buried in graveyards of earth and minds
Across this island-
Cudjoe too
In 1822
Deceased 1823
If you study what a name is meant to be
In our recent history
There was no identity of individuality
Your name said you belonged to somebody

[Some pirate from Waterloo
Marine Merchant etymology

I don't mean Marco Polo.
Sanitized their evil
And despised voodoo]

That we were not free.
So pride in a name could mean
We are blissfully unaware
How we really got here
And how our names came to be
[Imagine the irony of a house slave pulling rank on the field Negro!
'Massa love me!
Massa love me so!']

U

I

Yes,
That's ok,
Your thoughts you'll carry
As far as Grand Bay cemetery
And when they get bury
Doh worry
If is bad mind
It must return to take me
As big as dem manchineel
Stanley want to chop down
To plant fruit tree

Your thoughts big and mighty like
Pharaoh
(Whose name I don't know)
Everything for the living
We're taking in de Afterlife
Watch US
Sailing down de river
If they're as high as the water
In the Aswan reservoir
When they burst from
The underground chamber
Ah bound to drown

So think plenty
Think of me
Think my status
Be happy
Swell up yuh head
And make plenty fuss

Thinking is free
But don't worry
We go sell and become millionaire
When you in de dust

II

Papa,
When you go down to the grave
You not going with a whimper
Nah Sah!
It would be good and proper
Loud
Clapping thunder
Proud
Like marching soldiers
Like the Egyptian Pharaoh
All your worldly goods
Would be taken with you

True,
You'll miss nothing
And nothing would miss you
People would see the sunset
And talk about you
As the after-glow
They would see you
Often
And be sure
You ent really dead
You juss go

Like over dey so
Behind the tree
Round the hill
Way they can touch

But you won't feel

Plenty fuss now
But no big deal
So many people
Will talk about you still

Deal?
This thing about coffin seal;
You'll be living doing plenty ting
Even making children
So don't worry with them who talking
Saying the dead knows nothing
King you is now
King you is
When you dead egain.

M

Africa finds division even
In the dispersion
Of her progeny
In these islands of the Caribbean
A name to which we don't belong
Strangers,
Even in the cemetery
(Common ground you'd assume)
I wonder
What did Marcus Garvey see
In the possibility of a return
Of Exiles to a home
In which they may not fit
With any certainty?
Unless we really
Can get away from the grip
Of the restricted view of many
Like among the congregated in the cemetery

RETURN TO THE VILLAGE

I

I returned to the village,
Arriving clueless
'What is this?
A manifestation of that which affects us as we age?'
The fences were broken, the concrete pavement unraveling,
The coralita rampant –the vines of death seemed – everywhere – dominant.
Accentuated by the dry season slant
Houses mourning lost occupants
Sheep foraging for bits in the drain...
It must be memories of better- a vibrancy greater
The absence of dilapidation
That induces this emotional pain

Then uncertain I became
'Are you sure?
Among ruins is always
Where we been living
Isn't this a story of evolution?
Or are we just seeking escape
To say so it was?
As if that justifies, exempts me from trying?'
'But what about the rusted barbed wire rolled with galvanized sheets
almost a year by the roadside?'
Eyesores, pollution of the neighborhood
True, I'm not lying.

I returned to the village
Thinking of the people I've forgotten
Victims of my exile
The past erased, glossed over
(I swear its two years since a perfect week on the sea!)
The perfection we knew

Around Easter
The endless days of August
Are now fewer and fewer

And new vistas to the shore have been opened
By bulldozing the field of manchineel-
Windbreak erased
(This was my village!
I feel the pain too!)
Mangroves became rotting skeletons
The lagoons silted
And the grand sentinels fell
Victims of a global warning
And that time is coming
When we would not be here again
And the village would still be new or decaying
Alive or dying
In the eyes of whoever is looking.

II

The 'Labours of Hercules'
Exposed ignorance anew
Ignited a compromised passion for an island review
That is why I engage in journeys afresh
Searching, scouring dry ravines, ridges with limestone outcrops
Forcing visual collections of pictures
Personal curation, collecting samples and paper documentation

The hills now clothed in green
[A matter of light absorption
Visual illusion outside the spectrum]
Dissected by pastureland
As if marching to the horizon

A sea now serene in the early morning
That was yesterday galloping to the shore
The clouds heavy set, pregnant with expectations
Soon their compulsory labour fulfilled
Beautiful release across and beyond her spinal prominence

But I remain far from satisfied
I insist that the majority
Escape beneath my mental radar
The significant displays undetected
They are simply too high
Despite conscious effort
Extended extensive sweeping to capture
Failing every time to paint a definitive portrait
Of this island
Not this year
And not ever.

III

In these isolated corners of stagnation
Contemplating the rows where trees stand
Spades, buckets, gravel, sand
Building walls, restricted communication

Where in recent times
No ideas have been born-
Apart from the old ones in reverse circulation
The whole island is like the sidewalk in town
Pavements of hewn stone from an era bygone;
At the headquarters the fence leans,
Falling down
Playing fields, Dumfries, Sabazan
Like a dump consuming prime agricultural land
Ingredients ripe for a revolution
The flag of surrender hoisted
We welcome the children of Tarleton

In these recesses of wired expectations
Who are we?
Where are we?
Like me!
You've got to face de book written by a new generation
Like a clash of culture and civilization
One and the same
But hear me sound blaring
Killing out the rhythms of the Big Drum
While we're on the outskirts
Taking in riddled wisdom
(Boats meet and pass
The time being one past one)
Different results if you change from addition to multiplication

You can hide the reality
And because we are so dumb!

On this 13 Square Mile Island
And beyond
Food for the Poor water desalination
Sand mining, tree chopping, land degradation
If you revert to pre-1974 identification
Older version of something better?
Or just jaded memory of older ones?

The paint is peeling
The lime trees are gone
We don't pick the cotton
Lands lie abandoned
But with whom do we compare?
Like boats we are passing
Sailing away by subtraction
On these isolated shelves
Do you understand?
Our real situation?

Drums A, B, C

Drum A- side

Like you,
I'm dedicated to my ignorance
Trapped in its resonance
Trying to imagine life in a world
I've never seen, been,
To understand art
Like devotees in galleries
Paying obeisance, making pilgrimages.
There must be something
I've been missing all these years

Drum B - middle

I loathe this poverty of mind
Poverty in my mind
Too poor to read

Too poor to lead
Poor on this earth
So poor I doubt my worth
Please, let me get to heaven first

I cannot fathom my resources
Critical thinking deserts my mind
Like I never studied the right courses
Economy, philosophy, Shakespeare
War of the Roses, Animal Farm
I'm A Want 2 Be Wannabee
I didn't even understand the Grenadian Revolution
I did not got the correct interpretation
I feel cheated like I'm living in some slum
My duly noted frustration
Nothing is right; everything is wrong
When you are poor as poor as I am
I'm just a pauper
I've got nothing to offer
It's scandalous!
Out of order!
I've got freedom
But didn't sound the expanse of my liberty
And it doesn't matter
How often I hear from Trevor
What has happened
Has already happened already
Fait accompli

August 1, 2016
Around 11: 50am
Belle Vue

Drum C

There was anger, violence and irritation -
Incomprehensible spitfire ammunition
In voices elevated- full oration
From the front and rear of the van
'Not you! Is not you we come to!'

On the day
When WE
The offspring of imprisoned hands,
Later called peasants [we are not from or of France!]
(Although our history embraces far greater complexity)
Continue to farm the right to continue poor
On the lower rungs of society's ladder...

They came not to praise Queen Victoria
Just to retrieve Lydia
And there was no irony in the evolution of history
That the progeny of owners and their property
Can ride in the horse drawn carriage as friends
(Who is the driver? Who is the passenger?)
And take it so far
(But how much has changed in our mentality?)

The divisions created
Unlike horses being broken
Whether in ignorant bliss
Or the viewpoints and anger we inherit
Surfaced in every utterance:
'We don't want you!
Is not you we come to!'

DE WURL BY YOU

If the world did know you
It woulda cry
No lie
Me boy
Recognize you
Just before you die
Because de world woulda be so missing you
No ifs, buts or maybe
You, who so important dey

You crazy!

I see
I thinking
How de world revolving
Down dey so
Just south of me big toe
Who could tell me no,
And say is how I have big ego?
No,
The world need me for sure
Oh, oh

Mmmh we
Me?
Dey say it have islands bigger than Grenada
Alive in the Essequibo River
Or that 2 billion and 1 people inside ah China
I don't really know
How or why didn't really matter
Not to me
Or my everyday
Watch!

I can't ever connect
Wid dem kinda thinking anyway
Because all I could see
Is the world around me

And who saying
Is head dey pushing
Trying to be sophisticated philosophizing
De world is right by dey nose
What else dey could be smelling?
Only Grenada put chicken
In peas and dumpling
Everybody else
Is one type of styling:
'Corn-pork', pigtail, salt-beef
The plantation pickled our genes and wings

So de world muss miss me
And realize a space blank
I is ah important man
The world have to give me thanks
And record me and play me
Like Peter Tosh and Bob Marley
Anything happen
De world must cry you know
And maybe you too
Nuh true?

THE 5TH ELEMENT SHORT

I

The fifth element
Rests by the lagoon
Feeding the near-shore reefs off Dunblane
With the silt of Belle Vue and La Resource
Wondering,
About all these men that came
Like Thomas William Bell Esquire
1877
Dead at Dumfries Monday 3rd
A September morning
Will it for us be the same?
That history has no bearing
On our destiny,
Future,
The fifth element
Or whatever its (real) name?

II
5TH ELEMENT EXTENDED
Dedicated to the 'free divers' of Mt.Pleasant

The fifth element was written
Like coming from a sea water tenement prison
An ignorant reason in pursuit of an elusive ocean surgeon
That disappears in the liquid labyrinth of its home

To surface
Like crystal bubbles
In the shadow of Sabazan
The flip side of Craigston
Adjacent to Dumfries
All these ones belonging to Scotland...

I'm drowning in history
Names, acres, land under cultivation
Hogs head, the Negroes' corn rations
Malvina Wells of Grand Bay
Help Me!
Even 1795 Julien Fedon
When there was forty to one
But no rebellion

The fifth element
Swims along a ledge
Keeping company with the edge
Lone shadow cast over
Patches of white sand
Like the blows of a sledge
Hammering my concern
I'm not the only one!
But I am!

III

The fifth element
Swims ashore to greet
Hugh Munroe
His son who died young
John Dallas subjecting Negroes
Pregnant wid chile
Blows!
Until chile come
And yet the taste
Of corned beef, pickled mackerel
Never left my pores
Just as massa never left these shores
When will I swim free?

The fifth element is unrelenting
Like tides

Rising and falling every six hours
Pulling,
Forces against which you cannot
Swim and win
Indigo grew
To dye me like seawater blue
In Grand Anse and Meldrum
But not again!
Look!
Now everything remains barren
But the Fifth Element

PRESIDING OFFICIALS

The men who preside over the degradation of an island
Would all live forever-long, long, long
Even as do those from a now distant era
Colonials bleeding profit
Only to abandon once dry
The past occupiers shaping an island's future

This time,
They separate more than land marked by bound stones*
We've got severed hearts and hands inside the same homes
And they are in every way
Merchants, profiteers, pirates in new masquerade
With followers in character of field slaves
And the peasants never rise
They just grin and behave

While men run riot
And divide up more plots
Before time runs out
And God comes
To take everything back
A solace of escape and hope
Defense mechanism to cope
Because they do as they want
Even long after they can't
And it will be ok that way.
* Boundary markers

RETURN FROM NY

'Joseph!'
'Look how many years it's been!
So beautiful to see you brother!'
I was classmates with his sister
Natasha
Suspended for three days
Over a contrived misdemeanor
(I didn't touch her!)

However,
Joseph,
New York,
That dissected borough
Glad to see you maan
What are you doing?
Happiness,
Seeking,
That is the dream.
True,
I too
Feel the same thing!
And the beard you're sporting
Mimicking Lebron?
Or making a statement
Like Jeremy Corbyn?
(So too my nephew Dane
Who keeps the company of a camera across America)

LOAFER BY BAIN

He was standing
Like a stranger
Lost by the well of water
Petite Bain*
And as for me
This could be
Before slave hunters came
To disturb the peace
Connectivity of the family
The community

Now we are standing
Watching the washing
In a world to which we lay no claim
We cry tears for sure
So strong
So fertile
But devoid of direction
Ideas-none
Mentally sterile
Opposite the outer profile
Generations bypassed, excluded, denied
Potential discarded without a try
Decomposing in the present
Of our hostility in this island territory
Of political immaturity

Leaving us behind
To shovel sand unto truck trays
And that's the life until
What's up with that?

As I'm helpless to help you,

Take you out of Tibeau
I can only lift you
In my poetry
To say
I see you
And every time I do
I anger over our destitution
Your position
My fear
That we soon will disappear
Before we become conscious of anything
* Village well built by Africans

GRIOT LORNA

Lorna from Union Island
Pure fire in she bosom
'Carriacou people like kakaroach
Imagine!
If it was we had a stadium!'

'And how you could bring a Grenadian
Who knows nothing about historical connections,
To walk on de jetty wand waving in hand
People can't get off the boat
And you call dat immigration!'

'Watch,
Ah woulda pick up de phone
And talk to de big man
Get her out from dey!
They stopping inter-island tourism
Asking for passport and ID
When half of Carriacou is Union Island
When you in Puerto Rico
Is America you land!

Lorna from Union
Speaking volumes
Griot African
'They stopping people from going to the beach
They sell out Canouan!'

So I wonder if they know
Who is Kayak and who is Vincy*
Free trade movement of people
That was always how it used to be
If it happening in Carriacou

Grenadines people dey
Is one big family
But Kayak people like
They don't support the same way
*Native of St.Vincent and the Grenadines

II

All yuh
Ent know nutton in Carriacou.
Instead of all yuh unite,
Spending time
Cutting down trees
And fighting people
Like all ah all yuh not from de same family
African black people
Yuh ever hear more!

Learn from Mansa Musa
Trod the Sahara
On pilgrimage to Saudi Arabia
The Emir of Kano, get to know
Possibilities and so much more
The island is beautiful
Why not keep it like a garden?

Instead
All Yuh
Prepare to fight
Spite and victimize
When we evaluate the value
Way we go reach
How far we go go?

ZAGADA PRINCIPLE

Is Joe who
Remember
The neigbour
Asking Sherman
With accosting derision,
'So, Thief man, what's your intention?
What you going to do
With your nocturnal lumber collections?'

And he was ready for she.
'Ah going to build a skyscraper
Just like the ones you see in America
So when ah up dey
And look down on you and you children
All you appear on de ground
Like Zaggada.'*
'You get you answer?'
* Ground lizard

RESIGNATION

Is this a copout?
The easy route out?
Or a wisdom so high
Few can easily access
In broad daylight,
To perceptive scout?

We've been left to carry the burden
Too heavy for us to negotiate
We've been believing in forever,
Forever,
And don't know how these links to sever
But you demand it from us everyday
With bombardment
The reproach
The new morality
Ethology
And we're supposed to adjust
Retract, reform
Give way...

And the laws you lay
Suddenly
We've regressed into backwardness
In your estimation
All our legal statutes
Issues
We send you for final arbitration
So,
Shall we confront this uncertain future
In isolation
On our own
And maybe saddled with sanctions?

Help us with this confusion

We're not talking of Mr. Evolution
He is ok
And can hold his ground
We find it funny too
That the main protagonists
Turn to chants from their zoo
To make the opposition feel common
Less than human
Isn't that ironic!
That they ridicule their deity!
Forgetting where they came from?
No,
We not into acceptance by majority
Peer pressure conformity
We feel free to believe what we want
But tell us,
Shall we cut you off completely?
And go our own way?
Before you change on us anew
And our uncertainty escalates?

DRUM 3

Lacatan

"The Nation Dance is ah spiritual thing, with deep meaning. Doh watch it simple so."

Big Drummer

An insurrection of the slaves in Carriacou was apprehended in September, their dissatisfaction being attributed by their owners to the teachings of the Rev. William Nash, the Anglican clergyman there; but a careful investigation by the Governor showed that the allegation was unfounded, and no trouble ensued. A good trade sprang up at this period between

One reference from 1806 in the Grenada Handbook

"You don't inherit something just to sell it."

G C Grosvenor, 6ᵗʰ Duke of Westminster

"The sale of land was something that was taboo; it was just something people didn't do."

Once upon a time in Carriacou

And after restoration of the great houses overlooking the sea
After its transformation into a marine conservatory
After imposition of restrictions on fishing for free
And after we didn't go to university to hold a degree in sea biology
and the science of thievery
And how we go live in the new economy?
If we ent ready?
Mmmnh. Mmmnh.
2016
Could be nearer to 1833!

NAH'S VISION

'Believe me fuh true
Ah get a vision
Ah was taken around de island
By an ole woman
Me family
Yu en know she?
Dey bring me by Dover
Leave me right dey
By a concrete structure
Me two hands up- in de air!
And ah say,'
"Way you mouth lead yuh
Is you behind have to pay!"

'Cousin Nah
Ah thought you did see farther
Way, way, past Gun Point* into the future
That the older heads woulda
Tell you way we is,
Way we going
And whaat wrong wid people in Carriacou.'
They might ah been poor
But the ancestors
Never live so
No,
Cutlass and hoe
Penny ah row
I help you
Hand in hand
Together until we all done
So go,
Get a new vision
Before we done
* According to official maps drawn up by the British, Carriacou's
northernmost point is part of St.Vincent & the Grenadines

HOPE FOR CARRIACOU
Inspired by Jill in Tief
I

He is coming on a horse
White
Riding
To bring down the curtain
On everything
All hopes and dreams
To judge the dead and the living
And to ensure the exploited
And poverty stricken get in on the American Dream
Greater scheme
It's for real
Why you think its imagining?

II
[Dave in Dumfries]

'You want a saviour?
They give you one.'
'Dave, who?'
'For you to believe,
The Illuminati Jeffrey,
You better believe me,
It's even on internet TV,
Check the channel
Conspiracy'

III

Who else would rescue Kayak People?
(I ask Patricia what to do)
['Wait for them to find you
Dig up archeology in Grand Bay

Ship the findings to Holland and the UK for recovery.
(What will we do with it here!)
The grave diggers will discover your paper
And scan it to see
You'll be famous posthumously
But the island would remain
Ok?']
And hold them before they fall through the back door
Unto the seashore
With nowhere to come back to
And nowhere to go
Must be the king
You know what ah mean?
He is coming soon
Morning, night or noon
To save us from certain doom!

Look how long
You been singing the same song
To explain the current situation
Desperation and inadequate education
To stand toe to toe with our demons
And challenge
Without having to run and back down
And in the name of the son
You rebuke Satan
Plead the blood
I'm not making funds
Just hold on
Til now
The classrooms
Do not see the history before and after 1983
Just how Kalinago jumped into the sea
Running from a lynch mob and band of tief
Who wrote the story and left us for posterity
Proudly we

Erect a monument
Because he is coming
Something like a hurricane
In a whirlwind to blow down everything
Sweep away the debris
Make the place clean
And I'll be waiting
To wake up from this dream
And let a whole new reality begin
Do you believe he is coming (too)?

IV
Inspired by Patricia

The money done!
We ent have none
And we lose the land.
Welcome!
To the land
From way we come
Where people live in love
All ah we is one
(Used to be)

Woe to you nonbelievers
Who believe the premature cannot survive without incubators
You should be more connected to your grand mothers
Bush tea to break the day
Leaven
Bread in brick oven
And cloth for diapers
Now a whole generation
Has lost faith
Cannot make the connection
That we are survivors
(*Black survivors*)

Hope to you skeptics
Who have lost the wisdom
The forefathers once kept
Despite tending cows
And rows of corn
While school was skipped,
Came out replete with common sense
And wisdom so deep...
Really?

V

Jeffrey,
Facebook
And popularity
Are not the essence
Of what it means to be owners of land
And then give it away for some money
These people know how to do without
Hungry belly and dry mouth
Saving shillings and pence
To buy wood and shingle
And erect on land they own
And they didn't need fence
Hence,
When would we leave behind the conceit and intellectual pit?
And believe
And see
And begin anew?

VI

I cannot
Not
Have hope
Just to cope

With the oscillations
To face the dawn

Same hope
I have for this island
And its survival.
You have to understand
That in every generation
There are the unsteady doubters
And of late,
Outright nonbelievers
(The people called monkeys are the last to believe in the theory)
But the island would triumph
In its own way
So don't despair
Have faith
And wait...

'Thomas Tarleton likely drew on raw cotton from his 509 acre Mount Pleasant plantation on Carriacou, worked by 227 enslaved Africans in 1790.'

Unknown Source

I

Dear John Tarleton Esquire,
I, a son of Aman, grew within distance of
Or upon your estate
(By what means was your acquisition made firm?)
On the ridgeline
Overlooking the expanse of Mt.Pleasant
And islands in the lake to the north

Liverpool, I've been told
Years many
1716, 1782, 1770
Bear no real meaning for me
I cannot imagine in 2016, I cannot bear
Although I feel better
For the coming of 1910
Or some say 1920, was the correct year

John,
(I may address you in the first person)
The guns still guard the headland
Dedicated to your fame.
So after these centuries
Your name resides and presides the same
So that descendants could resurrect the claim
Where horses and mules grazed
And 'your' Africans slaved
Miniature badlands riddle the ground
Washing its substance into the Atlantic basin

One thing,
As you are no doubt aware,
In reality
It's really part of a sea
A lagoon
With its reef
Nearing the land extension
Like so many memories
And gold coins
Lost in the sands of years-to-year....

II

For Trevor and sons

'We need to keep them settled in Bogles
The Negroes should never return to the house or chapel
To invoke on us their voodoo
Or use oleander to plant poison.'

WONDER TRANSFER

I wonder
What would happen
On a morning when it rained
The grass would be wet
Mud waiting for every step
To happen;
Would you
Have to leave the earthen floor
Made warm by your torso
To fetch the milk
Feed the pigs
The chickens
Fodder for the heifer and horses
Soaked without cover
Because that's just the way it is?

We live so far removed
From a world we don't know
It intercepts our imagination
Because we can't go back
And return to the past
While we're busy living one track

Did you leave your home by the sea
With all that pottery
To travel inland
To gather and farm?
Was there a lookout
A scout
To shout out a warning?
And when death visited
How did you explain?
Did you believe in another dimension?
Or that the dead could return in a resurrection?

We live
Off the sand on the seashore
Spades of brutality
Collecting dollar bills
Is so important
As we've come to know
Bones of the dead
We will truck that away too
That's why I ask the question
Because I really don't know

I wonder
What it was like in the 1920's
Working on the subway
In Brooklyn
(Switch, continents I'm changing)
Bring me back to Panama
And Maracaibo
Was it easy?
Cutting sugar cane
In Trinidad and Cuba?
Picking fruits in Florida
And refining oil in Largo?
And when you sent the
Cheque and money order
To put in the bank
And buy a few acres
Did you imagine
Them ungrateful grandchildren
Would sell it out
For a wink
Without a blink?

We live
Consumed by evolution
Everything explained

Except the Grenada Revolution
But I try to see
Try to understand
What you gave to me
Where I'm coming from
Maybe I would trod easily
Find purpose
Avoid the trauma

But I don't know
So that's why
I wonder
And ponder
Life on the plantation
The mutilation and beatings
Deprivation and terror
Freedom and our burdens
Now we can be whatever
History doesn't mean a thing
It doesn't matter
So I keep asking the questions
I really wonder

INFIDELS

We should be among the infidels
People without belief
For whom the only relief
Is the grave
Bearing no responsibility for our atrocities
The inequalities of society
We take no credit for the origins
Only mark our trail in it
For the minority benefit
We prefer to be among the infidels

And who de hell can say
Preach a sermon to displace us
From our perch?
Plus
Forget the uneducated passion of ignorance
Proliferating among the believers
Living in slums and around shanty towns
They can wait and pray
And dream
For god to come
We prefer to be
Rulers of the economy
And remain infidels until that day

I'll sell you everything
You want to buy
For the right price
But I don't know big money
So how much would you give me?

Tell you
The truth man

Is just a piece ah land
And dem children in Brooklyn and England
Feel no particular connection
Wid history or the current situation
They forget what happen
"No Irish!
No dogs!
No black man!"

And don't worry
About Jacob
(He dat extend de farm)
Or Zimbabwe
Or whoever it is
That the objectors worship
Or pedestalize as examples in hope
(Evolution will triumph
In this life at least)
So buy
Come quick
Before Carriacou done finish!

SORTIES OF TEARS

The vultures have been circling
Patient sorties across the near heavens
Without release
In anticipation of carcasses on the plane.
In the meantime, the lord is coming
Like lightening out of a clear blue sky
Streaking toward the earth
And there will be carcasses
Some will live
But we're all going to die

The drums are thumping
Coming over and across the way
The sound of something earth shattering
Meaning no one can stand in its way
In the meantime,
The faithful are praying
Hoping that their gods would hear what they say
There will be blood in the field
Tears in the hills
But don't believe a word that they say.

STRANGER WHO?

Well hi and hello there,
Where please are you coming from?
West Virginia?
Alabama?
Mississippi?
But, is that deep in the heartland?
Are you under a flag?
(West Indians in Brooklyn
Display theirs in cars and vans)
Cross of Saint George?
Or the 7 State Confederate?

Have you heard?
That the world is now One?
Freedom to move
Choose
But only for some?
Amidst fenced borders
Jungle camps and discrimination
13 Square Miles?
Where?
A Haven without verification?

Can we really be friends?
Or would there be transplanted divisions
And a new economy
To add to the legacy of slavery?

Control in totality
Residents Above All
Retreat to undisturbed seclusion
To calypso, not a fan
But

No derision living the motto
"I want a plantation."*

What's your opinion?

Hi,
Hello,
I don't know...
Should I be the stranger in this town?
Should I import tour guides and my historians?
If this was your town?
Would you allow it to happen?
Could I see the light?
Or was my whole life darkened?
So now how come?
What is this?
Who are you?
Where are you coming from?
And what is your mission?

* Sung by Barbadian John King

ELEGY FOR ME

I'll be writing my elegy
Without any hypocrisy
Not so far removed from Grand Bay
And say
Can you hear me?
Can you hear me?

I'll be covered in brown earth
Tainted by white nearing the rock
And for what it's worth
I'll be hearing the slow moving chains
Early in the morning
And I'll be singing,
'What did I do to you
Oh Carriacou!'

COMMISSION TO THE ARTIST

Dearest Nichole,
Of course, I remember you!
The absence of a mention in my diary
Has no bearing on the reality behind school doors
I now write to invite
Because of conversations on the radio
Words in collision so foreign to me:
"Indulgence in colour fields,"
"Looming Black Presence,"
"Cultural Vigour,"
"Abstract Impressionism,"
And accompanying lexicon

There is Canute* of course
But you are my contemporary
Artist with brush
With whom I share familiarity

I am sorry about this late realization
And even so,
It's only through contrived circumstances,
I neither went to school nor completed study
I dwell way outside the periphery of the art society
To recognize your vision
And a talent different
Seriously Nicky
Our class was never ready for your emergence
So soon after 1983

Does that in any way explain your departure?
Did it frustrate your creativity?
To be among people like me, so lacking in sensitivity?
Unwilling to celebrate and embrace
With vibrancy
Your oddities?

This island barrier!

You've joined the exodus
Of intellectual exiles
We think we are in fields of clarity
But it's a lie!
So I present you a commission
Backed by our shared classroom foundation
To help me paint
Bestow depth, character

I'm frustrated
Still cannot grasp the lingo
Unable to pretend too
So please do
If only a return
To help me paint this portrait of Carriacou

* Canute Calliste, Carriacou's renowned painter

I

I too
Want to try me hand
At writing dead people a song
Before too long gone
Filled with expression
Rich with meaning
Overflowing with symbolism
I'm on
Riding
Writing
On de dead people bandwagon

Me mother say,
'Don't wait til ah dead to cry
Crocodile tears in yuh eyes
And buy expensive coffin
When you didn't used to
Give me nutton
You ole good fuh nutton
If ah wish you
It bound to take you.'

I want to go far back
Write to a Carib and Arawak
Tell dem we lose track
If they could come back
In Dumfries, Sabazan, Belle Vue and Grand Bay
But the land way all yuh used to stay
Disappear

I have nothing to do
With Craigston or Prospect
Or writing letters to dead Europeans
Me have no paper

Enough ships to carry
Or sufficient stamps...
Your children still come here
And do as they want
License to walk
Fence the beach
Claim the mangrove
Say how we nice
To then tell us we can't
And since the Revo
Everybody like dey stunt

Then
Miss C boys and dem
*Tufia malewez**
Ah curse dem!
Bring back Anansi Cudjoe
Play drums on dem
Beat dem!
Drive dem away!
Loose dem!
And bury!
The earth swallow
De land condemn

Ah want to write ah song
About Carriacou
Fuh true
Plenty lines
Riffs fuh so
Bridges and more
To give you the idea of what happen

The land is fuh people
And dat is way
The dead does go

But ah not so sure
How much time
Left to go
When it will be no more
So ah riding the wagon
Writing ah dead people song
So when de dead hear it
De dead would understand.
*An expression of severe malediction; wretched.

II

It make me ent want to dead here self
Fuh dem to make greedy over drink
And look to joge# food away
Take away

For 'Doctor'

'I'm telling you,
True,
Life in Gambia
No different to Carriacou.
When you arrive
Is ah joy
Everybody so happy to see you
Light a fire
Roast a breadfruit,'
'Our children have returned
Home!'

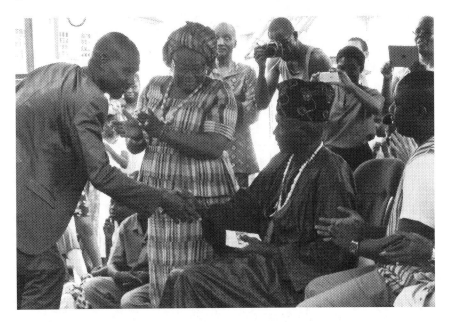

Meeting Paramount Chief Bia Bureh

On the Occasion of the Temne Reunion
Carriacou and Sierra Leone, 27/9/16

MIDDLE PASSAGE 2016
TEMNE REUNION

Reflections of a slave child

This my reefs
These my shallows
This my currents
This my passage
Through the deep
Where tides run
And tides sweep

The ocean is my solace
Oh my history!

This my journey
The middle passage
Did so much damage

But now I gather myself
A child restricted
By geography
The diet fed to me
Salted rations
Weighing me down
Denying my chance of return
Oh my middle passage!
Ever so often
I revisit scenes of your carnage

I am Temne
Bunce Island
Bondo Society
King Bai Bureh
But how did I get here,
On this plantation,
Separated from my family,
My clan?
And to see
That after more than 250 annums
You found me
Oh Temne
Temne Oh
Did you know
Despite the separation by water
And our insignificant number
Ever so often I would think of,
Remember Africa?
Sierra Leone, Ghana, Gambia
Cote d' Ivoire

So welcome!
To this my beach
This my sand
This my street
This my drum
400 years of loneliness
Exile and deliberate isolation...
Now here my family
Greet me!
Our reunion!
Don't you understand,
That middle passage
Could not erase the image?
Temne
Oh Temne oh
I hope you accept my message

REFUGEE

I have no citizenship
But I aint no refugee
Didn't arrive here by boat
But my forefathers came by sea
Now I got a passport
They want me to report to the Border Agency
Why can't we just live free
Like the Most Def Yassin Bey?

I didn't traverse the Sahara to reach these shores
Didn't drift or hit the rocks on Isla Lesbos
I aint from Syria, I already gat my Homs
I want to be free to paint my pictures
And not be a Banksy clone

I could be a child not born in Nauru
Just like you
I didn't make the current situation
So what you want me to do?
Remember, you were once a castaway lost at sea
Now you say I can't be free
To walk the bush around Sydney
Because I'm no Aborigine
(How ironic you want to be?)

I am a refugee
Temne
Sierra Leone
Child of an African
To Gambia
Fleeing Freetown
So when my brothers
On ships of distress

To America were flown
Express their concern
I don't resist
I must get to know where they're coming from

Because we're all refugees
Escaping some condition
Looking for freedom
Who will help us?
Please?
Who will hold our hands?

I have no citizenship
I am no refugee
I sometimes live in the Gaza Strip
And the West Bank Territory
But in today's world
It could be anywhere
Because One World
And Global Village
Are mere words
Up in their air,
'Stamp my passport
Give me the all clear!'

TEARS IN AMERICA
AND FROM D' USA

Land of the Free, Home of the Brave. But we become truly, only when we rest in the grave:

Minnesota Lights Out in Charlotte

I

You feel
That poor me in Carriacou
Could have any bearing on the things you do
In your city?
At the intersection
Draw your gun
Three shots
Another three
Blood will come down!
No man!
Who am I
Who I am!
Live streaming
My blood is screaming
Like Abel's did for Cain
'Sir! What did you do!'
Murder is murder
Mob execution
Or public lynching
It's all the same!

No man
What have I done!
What have you done!

Administrative leave
With pay
Brings no justice to me
What about freedom?
Abraham!
Our father!
Where is the liberty!

Believe me
I'm still living in chains
Slavery
Keep calm
While the law
Establishes
Circumstances
Investigation!
I'm dead
The Bounty Hunters walk free.

Minnesota!
Oh no never!
Minnesota!
Baton Rouge
Your bloody sister!
If you ever had feelings for me
I would see
Rivers
Blood!
Pools
Blood!
'I'm gonna die
Oh my God!'
But, he is yours only!

And yet you would not deny me opportunity to pray
II

Oh my Charlotte
North Corolinita
I remember
The Funeral of your sister Virginia
What a lament was raised on the shoreline over!

Although I never walked her sands
My eyes greeted many of her waters
Marshland and brown ocean
Plied by crab fishers
Until my return to this island

But now
What is this I hear of you?
Have you courted company
With bad people?
Didn't he?
Or did he have a gun?
Must it be
Every time we meet
Blood of one must run?
Oh my dear Charlotte
What if it was your son?
Or was he one?
Excuse the distance, the ignorancy
I too could be a gullible victim
Of circumstances
History,
However, I write to say to you
Just as we here in Carriacou
Wish for better days
Just down the road
Up ahead
Across the stop lights
Although frankly
The view is somewhat hazy
We can't nearly see the way
But we live in hopes...

Inspired by events of 8ᵗʰ November 2016

HAIL THE DON!

Now that the end has come
With the triumph of the Don
This is an invitation
For all Kayaks
To run
Come down
Come back home
And build skyscrapers
Farm the land
So we could export to Florida
Oranges, pumpkin
Cassava, water melon and green plum

Long time
She's been waiting
For something
Like this to happen
From Magna Carta
The arrival of the Pilgrims
To Pearl Harbour
The Cold war, Desert Storm
And Edward Snowden
Now the prophecy is revealing
Hail the Don!
And make America Great
Again

Hear ye!
Hear ye!
This is the triumph of democracy
Power to the people
And the right to choose

If Black Lives Matter
Then my Brother,
What have you got to lose?

Hail the trumpet sound
And let it rebound
As far as the graveyards of Canouan
We'll build the wall
Turn things around
We will be the best
Pound for pound
In Pasadena
And Old San Juan
Enter the new era
She will be great again!
All hail the Don!

'THE SUN WILL RISE!'

The sun will rise
In the morning
And until it burns out
That's how it will be
How it has always
So cheer up my brother
If your feelings are important
So too the
Two billions in China
And this is not a meme
The sun rises in the east
For you
As it rises for all of them.

The sun doesn't care
Who is in the Black House
Who built it
If there are cockroaches, rats, or a mouse
On or below
The couch;
Human proclamations
Predictions
Or word of mouth
The sun sees
Mt.Fuji
After and horrors of slavery
And guess what?
The sun
Didn't change its route

So of course
The sun will rise
No matter the State of the Union

The feelings in your heart
The sun doesn't even rise
It's earth's revolution
And it remains
Essentially hot
So you better cheer up...

Love him
Or loathe
The sun will rise
If you swear
Never to ever go there
Again
The sun will rise
No surprise
If you didn't read the emails
Or listen to the FBI's
Reprise
The sun doesn't care
Oh dear
Look E here
Even if you are a Bajan
The sun will rise

No matter your residency or colour
Brooklyn projects
Or suburbia Arizona
The sun will rise
Sometimes
It feels stronger
Heat
More fire
The sun will rise
So you better
Swallow your medicine
No matter how bitter

And cheer up
My brother
Keep your head up
Because the sun will rise
Regardless of your view
Of who
Yes
The sun will rise
No matter what.

Carriacou Chiffone
(Breakaway)

'You must open the ring with the Sponsor's Nation Dance. Later on, when the ring opens, you free to play anything and anybody can enter.' **Kayak Drummer**

"Mr. Knight also expressed himself as quite disgusted with the slowness and disinterestedness of the people on the island. I don't know how good a commissioner he will be, but he will certainly try to improve things for the people. Mr. Simmons listed the products of the island as cotton, peanuts, limes, onions, coconuts, yams, pigeon peas, mangrove oysters, and fish."

Richard E Blackwelder Field Notes, 1936

"I am grateful every time you come on to the Big Drum and transform from human to rhythmic artistry." **Poetic Duty I, 2013**

CARRIACOU BREAKAWAY

T

In Carriacou you dey we!
Like you ent know!
Wah you trying to play?
Youths want to study psychology
Yes, Carriacou people head need head repair
What is dis pre-occupation wid money?
Who get money
Plenty
They don't want to share undivided property
Everybody want dey deed individually

And what wrong wid dat
If it's the face of modernity?
Evolution
We can't remain as monkey
House?
Car?
You want tings to remain the same way?
Saraca?
Tradition?
It dying away?
Kayak people nuh easy
Money jumbie dey soul take way?
Somebody getting rich?
Really?
Somebody smart?
Silly!
Everybody don't care
Suspicion
Dividing society
Everybody righteous
Everybody need redemption
Everybody see everybody
Through eyes of jealousy
Nobody gets salvation
Talking behind back
Giving information to strangers free

In Carriacou yuh dey we!
Wah you tink!
Wah you expect!
Yuh tink dis is Englaaan
Wah yuh want to change dey?
Ress yuh self ah say
Like yuh ent know
Anything about Carriacou!

E

Tell ah man
Tell ah woman
Is the way it's done
On this island.
Everyone
Have an opinion
Without verification.

You didn't know
That is why they have Parang?
Beat people name
Like ole pan
Plenty bangarang
You didn't know?
Well let me tell you
What happen...

A

De I,
Yuh see
Like how yuh riding donkey
Same fuh we
Basic
Dust in de road
Twice ah year
Fix it
Rain come
Wash it
Bulldozer
Dig it
Pay some trucks
More dirt
Spread it

Basic

Yes I
Like how yuh is farmer
Since yuh eye register
In agriculture
Corn, peas, groundnut and cassava
Basic
What future?
You study in Guyana?
Fly to China?
Jungle?
Yellow River?
What do you?
You mad oh wah?
That's it
Keep it basic!

R

GONE FOREIGN

On this small island
Where we live
A life of imported imitations
Wholesale consumerism
Even our Big Drum exportation
Is gift-wrapped
Re-told and resold
So the stories we told
Could be interpreted for us to understand
And we readily purchase
The books of recipes
Dictated by experience
Catalogued on shelves
In the library of our oral history

The standards we strive to surmount
Are designed
In capitals
Far removed
But we have no choice
To be at liberty to choose
And there be no alternative strategy
So as to say
'Here,
Drink this
Bush tea
To start your new day.'

And where is our god
To whom we shall pray?
Find him in foreign

But how do we get there,
To bring him near?
Or maybe we just miss
That life is symbiotic
In its relationships
While some make it;
Others just eat

Every island doesn't need
To be original at all
Room for all
City dwellers
And the desert nomads

So don't condemn
This isle
As if
It is sterile
When residents
Of foreign
Keep coming
For piece of its peace
And Inhabitants
So docile
Homes in locations
You can hide from
Inside and outside investigation

S

'And if you have it
What does that mean?
Your life would be renewed?
Or wouldn't be the same again?
People would think special of you
Treat you like you're really somebody?
All of a sudden you'll be in the frame
of fame?
But what does that mean
If you have it
But it's not even playing?'

'It means,
I've got Controversy
1981
I can make conversation history
Like Prince and Sheila E
Musical chemistry by the NPG!'

But who cares
About what you know?
Where you've been
Who you've been to see?
Life is in your box
Limited mobility.
The world is not going to change for you
Sorry,
The world is not going to change in a hurry.

'But I don't live in the world!
I live in Carriacou!
Just so that you know!'

O

You should come to the garden
Sitting behind the wall
In front the road
And pretend to be a gardener
Farming words
As you observe how manure from the donkey
goats and ewe
Spur the basil and tomato.
Feel the joy off the vines of sweet potatoes
Observe the black bees
Buzzing between the trees
As a mellow cacophony drifts and lifts you
Digging, trying to unearth
Word-bearing fruit in the garden

F

I have these imaginations
Of perfection
Like a day on the beach
Just beyond Sabazan
I see the white cliffs
I see the protected indentations
In a cove
Where the wash covers
The white sand, pebbles, stones
Swishing, gentle interactions
When the tide is low
As the moon is high
And there is no separation
Between us islands
Everything is clean
As can be seen
Without interruption

D

I

When as boys
We fished the coves of Sabazan
As the sun goes down
In retrospection
I wonder
What were we doing?
Apart from sprats jigging
For bait
Listening the echo of waves sounding out
Hollow passages
Booming sounds akin to
Miniature hauntings
We waited for a tug, a run, a pick up
Waited dry
Then wet
Repeat desiccation
By the wind
What were we doing?

[Some time later I encountered Edwin
He ventured, 'You upstart!'
A word I associated with Marcus
And the UNIA
'That pompous Negro from JA'
Whatever that means
It's the same intonation
We are nothing,
No one,
So we can be treated to someone's Derision
OH CARRIACOU!
I'M A FISHERMAN
ON YOUR SHORE IN SABAZAN!

Bag of Money*
Would descend from Mt.Royal
(Beside the tower;
Legend on the map - a radio antenna)
Net slung,
Sweeping over head and shoulder
To collect the silvers
Shadows beneath water
Fill our buckets
Instead of collection by singular
But what were we doing?
Were the lessons
For life?
As suggested by James Son
From his Island and Beyond?#
Did we make connections?
Because I can't remember having a plan
The plan was fishing
Snapper, cavalli, mackerel, gar
And today,
It's just the same
The trucks, driven by men, still carry away the sand
While the solitary bridge has disappeared from its station.

*Nueley Dick, who later stated preference for the moniker, Bag of Dust
#Autobiography of James Mitchell, former PM, St. Vincent & Grenadines.

II
Oct 19, 2016*

Around 6:30
Am in the morning
There is an east wind now
Stronger than yesterday's incarnation
The sea's agitations agree
Sand grains the surf; a milky suspension

Sands in the surf
Surf in the sands
The clouds draped across the stage of the eastern horizon
Way beyond the prominence of the headland
Before the sun's grand entrée lifts, shifts the scenery

The east wind will blow a while
The grangojays- kamikaze pilots
Precise 90 degree plunges
Picking off sprats and silvers
Chased by larger predators
The waves dance to the truncated reefs
Lining the beach
Tumbling, falling, velocity decreasing
Retreating to gather themselves to come again.
I'm ready now to begin
Feet kiss the water
While the east wind blows

* And there be no irony in the way
This day escaped without fanfare,
Wholesale commemoration,
Particular attention.
Just another day.
As it began and ended
In 1983.

R

Who say we should leave de village!
Who say we need more knowledge?
Who sail to Europe and return so savage!

Suppose we happy?
To live in peace with we piece?
Suppose we analyze and realize

What they seek
We have it already?

Don't assume
Don't presume
Don't run from your identity to
Acquire emotional poverty
Become an intellectual refugee
Because you never belonged there!

Pretend sophistication
Make you look alien
Forget the world beyond
You've never been
Never seen
This is it- live within your limits

U

We're in the backyard
Coming through the back door
What da yah know
If you play Kendrick Lamar
I begin to think ghetto
It don't exist around here though
Why do we claim heritage we don't know?
Play me some Big Drum
To tell the story
Of yesterday's pain and sorrow
TEARS
And hope for tomorrow
This island won't remember me
But I will remember CARRIACOU for sure.

M

BUCKET OF HOPES

It is like this bucket I carry
Collecting from trees
Fruits nearing the corners of maturity
And others already there

I try to separate, grade, according to elasticity
When suddenly!
I was arrested by the distillation of a constituent fraction

I've got no solution!
The more I collect, the more my confusion
No reference I am! To you or for anyone!
To cling to, as a guide to
What should happen to Carriacou

I am a collector of rocks and driftwood
Times and its passengers
Samples of frustrations
Scattered in the furrows of my farmland
Looking for a Nobel ovation
But fulfilled if I achieve some satisfaction

So I write; pretend historian
I record voices, their stories
Stone Age, pre-historic picture-taking man.

With my axe and bows, leather pouch
Now a plastic bucket
But I feel no great leap of evolution
I am stunted, stumped, defeated
Resisted to carve out a definition of this island

PRELUDE TO TEARS OF THE DRUM
For Winston Ackee

Rastafari Cha Chai,
This morning when I hear the news about De I,
Bring to me mind, and tears to me eyes
The times,
The izzez,
The prayers,
De I Engine, Guamba,
Idee, Della, Mehgee, Master,
The pumpkins, squash, water melons;
Working the open ground,
Acres and acres, more than 40
And the juvenile protection
Living education, received from De I dem on de farm-
Potato in ash warm by cattle dung.

And we wouldn't burn down the fruits of 'Babylon'

Overstand
We just can't forget them things
In the life of this island
Despite the short life span
We keep moving on
And will remember the Dread
Now that De I is gone

Yeah man

And as I was trodding
To the beach this morn in the light of the rising sun
Holding a soft meditation of golden reflection on strains of the
Burning Spear Declaration:
'Jah protect De I
In De I going out and coming in,
Accident include...'

TEARS OF THE DRUM

As A memory of Selwyn 'Guamba' Andrew

I

If every man is entitled to his view
There is me, of course, you too
All the same
We came not to praise nor bury Caesar
Or offer any apology
Just to say:
There would be gallons of rivers
When the Drums play.

And WE don't care
If you believe in His Majesty
Or carry your own philosophy and Deity
All we got to say IS:
There would be Gallons
When the drums play
Tears through the years
Galvanizing emotions, captivating joys, releasing fears
We face it in our weakness
Mortality, final days
And all we got to say IS:
There would be tears by the Gallons
Across stony ground, pastureland,
TEARS on the beach, soaking through black and white sands
TEARS with the roll of every drum
Bass, Bula, Cut,
The pins must sound, resound
Vibrate, consume then relate the tone

Echoing across Ravine
As they lay me down
The honey from the orchard becomes bitter
The bees fly a final swarm
Camoon turns desolate
Because my brethren
TEARS will flow for so as I go home
Because when you look for me
I'll be long gone.

II
Wake night- Prospect Hall, 20/10/16

Burn dem with the Holy Spirit
Invoke feelings like a fire Baptist
Because we didn't lose it on dem slave ships
It was reborn every time
We live it,
In Big Drum
As we do in this wake for Selwyn
No matter the years in Brooklyn
The lights might flicker but never go dim

De conservative resist
Saying we can't do this- not in Jesus name
But when you see Ven
Lift her hands to the heaven
Who is she calling- on whose name?
For release, help,
'Carry my burdens
My God, to call on you cannot be in vain'
Power enough to sustain
If we get this memorial wrong
Forgive our history
As we intend to do it again and again
When you been through trials

Like we have
It could have been worse
All of us could have been lost, drowned
Or come across the river insane
So leh we dance and sing
Is all we have, nobody to blame
Raise ah praise song
Drown this sorrow
Until we do it again.

III

This night reminds of our space
In this firmament
Look at the faces!
Look at the stories!
The connections unexplored
It is not what you think it is.

Our fathers were here once
Now we hold temporary stay
Nursing this tradition of keeping
Our recently departed alive in our collective memory
And there is comfort in knowing we won't be forgotten
When our turn comes
The new generation will treat us the same way
So, burn dem with more Holy Spirit
Sing de chorus like you really mean it!

IV
21/10/16

And we will eat and forget
That it would be thus
On the day of our death
We need no reminder lest we forget

If it's not reached you
All it means is-
Not just yet

'We want chicken,
Give us,
Put some rice and peas
One more spoon please.'

It's communal; no reservations
Or claims of entitlement
And I want to say something
Over the froth excitement
Of the Heineken you're drinking
Happy hour after funeral...Irreverence?
Joke you making!
We celebrate the dead
Even as we do the living
If you have nothing to add
I beg you keep your holiness within
There will be no smoke, fire or lighting
But origin from the wood to cook these servings
For we the living that are now alive and remain
If you agree
Then say amen in Jesus name.

Inspired by Alexis of California
I

No, I've never been to America
Only Brooklyn- if you know what I mean
Is a Carriacou people ting
Working in the subway
Life underground
Between the East River and Manhattan

But California (ha ha ha)
Golden Gate Bridge
San Francisco and cable car
Wah!
Sacramento
Vineyards of Napa
It's like a replay of form-one geography
Climates of the Mediterranean
And redwood sequoia

II

Glad you came
To influence a change of view ever so slightly
Who wouldn't feel attracted the first time they came?
Naturally,
The way we see the world, there is always another possibility
Like in California; one time in Mexico
Alaska, now a Stranger in Moscow
And we too share commonality
At least in name
In the hills of Belair

LEAVE CARRIACOU!

You can go to Panama
Dig some dutty
Gather some earth with Marcus Garvey

Carriacou small-13 Square Miles
You must look outwards
Not within and stay backwards

Pass Venezuela
Leave behind
Not only a son and daughter
But also,
Display your mark as
A knowledge collector

It often gets insular
When you're on all sides surrounded by water
So leave it behind for yonder
Elevate the mind... more power.

Read a verse
Script a chart
So many books in the world
Where to start?

Embark on the journey of your discovery
Like the day I greeted Lemn Sissay
To be transported to somewhere in Ethiopia
And in Gambia spending the day by the sea
Carriacou small, don't just stay dey
And think you know everything
Like how ground dove
Claim to know everything already...

LIFE LESSONS

Yes Sir,
I'm sorry to say
I only thought of
Telling you thanks before today,
Today.

Anyway, you wouldn't mind...

So thank you for the insight
Before my time
To years like 1949
When you returned from the bay early
To begin your first day as headmaster
And forgot-sent the strap un-scraped to Sophia
Ha ha
The fish returned furnished the reminder-
Life lessons live with us forever.

Sophia [Brathwaite née McLeod] and son Nicholas

*Sir Nicholas Brathwaite of Mt.Pleasant, and cousin of Malco, died on 28 October 2016. He was buried at sea on November 9, closing a chapter, and this collection.

Drum Note:

MABI (Ibo clan): And thank you for the edit-fication by tel-eye-vision. This is my river. This, my flood. This, my tears by the gallon.